IS JOHN 3:16 THE GOSPEL?

IS JOHN 3:16 THE GOSPEL?

David Pawson

Terra Nova Publications

Published in Great Britain by
Terra Nova Publications International Ltd.
Orders and enquiries: PO Box 2400 Bradford on Avon BA15 2YN
Registered Office (not for trade): 21 St.Thomas Street, Bristol BS1 6JS

Cover design by Roger Judd

ISBN 978 1 901949 55 1

Printed in Great Britain by
Creative Print and Design Group
Harmondsworth

PREFACE

This book is based on a series of talks. Originating as it does from the spoken word, its style will be found by many readers to be somewhat different from my usual written style. It is hoped that this will not detract from the substance of the biblical teaching found here.

As always, I ask the reader to compare everything I say or write with what is written in the Bible and, if at any point a conflict is found, always to rely upon the clear teaching of scripture.

David Pawson

Contents

PREFACE   5

1 GOSPEL IN A NUTSHELL?   9

2 WHAT'S IN A WORD?   19

3 THE GOD WHO KILLS   47

4 TEACHER IN THE DARK   61

5 THE MESSAGE FOR CHRISTIANS   75

6 APOSTLE OF WRATH   91

POSTSCRIPT AND PRAYER   95

1

GOSPEL IN A NUTSHELL?

In my library there is a copy of a book entitled *The Gospel in Four Thousand Languages*. When you open it, you find one verse, John 3:16, translated into four thousand different languages! This is the best known verse in the New Testament – perhaps in the whole Bible – and many people think it is a good summary of the gospel. It is certainly one of the very few verses for which most Christians can give the chapter and verse reference.

For God so loved the world that he gave his only begotten Son, that whoever believes in him shall not perish but have everlasting life.

Called by some the 'golden text', it is often referred to as 'the gospel in a nutshell'. Like most preachers, I have used it as a text for a sermon. But I have to confess now that, like most Christians, I totally misunderstood the verse. I remember some of the alliterative titles I gave each section when I preached on it. I began with the 'largest love' and I went on to the 'greatest gift' and then the 'direst danger', finishing up with the 'longest life'. I can remember bits of the sermon from years ago, but alas I will never be able to preach it again. Once you discover the true meaning of a verse, you can never go back and use it with a wrong meaning again. So I am warning you now that I may spoil John 3:16 for you for the rest of your life. But I hope that this book will also give you the true meaning of what is a wonderful message, and a very important one, especially for Christians.

So we use John 3:16 primarily as a gospel text. I am sure you know the cliché 'a text out of context is a pretext'. Regrettably, it can also be used as a 'proof text'. Because at one point the Bible was divided up into chapters and verses, and each verse was given a number, there is a tendency to treat the Bible as a box full of proof texts. We think that, if we can find one text that says what we want it to say, then we have given proof from the Bible about a particular view or position. John 3:16 has been used like that, out of context. I believe it is one of the most mistranslated, misunderstood and misapplied verses in the Bible, as we shall see. I have had to study it in much greater detail than I have ever done before, because I have been receiving a number of emails and letters asking one simple question: 'What about John 3:16?' For the last year or two, I have had an increasing burden that we have made a major mistake to focus our gospel preaching on the *love* of God. That may come as a bit of a shock to you until, I explain what I mean by that. For the last hundred years, gospel preaching has begun with the love of God. In a nutshell, we have preached to unbelievers that God is love, that he loves everybody, and therefore that he loves *'you'*, the individual unbeliever. We have focused on the love of God as the *primary message* that we have for the world. The good news is God loves *you* and wants *you* to know that and wants *you* to accept that love. But the truth is that the apostles never talked like that!

Particularly troubling is the phrase that crept in about twenty years ago, 'the unconditional love of God'. Recently I asked those in a large Christian gathering to put their hands up if they had heard this expression, 'the unconditional love of God'. More than three-quarters of those present indicated that they had already heard it. I then asked: 'Would you put your hand up now if you have found that phrase in your Bible.' Of course, nobody responded to that. So where did we get it from? We have picked it up, and it is a most misleading phrase. The adjective 'unconditional' can mean a whole lot of different things.

When it is said that God's love is unconditional, it is implied that he loves everybody *just as they are*. That is how that phrase comes across to unbelievers. God's love is 'unconditional', which means therefore that he does not judge people. He loves them just as they are — so come to him just as *you* are. Whatever happened to the word 'repent' — a word which actually means 'change'?

The first step in coming to God, the very first step, is to change, to *repent*. But the phrase 'the unconditional love of God' says, 'Come as you are.' A real burden in my spirit began to develop, and I began to ask radical questions about preaching the love of God – especially 'unconditionally' – to unbelievers. If we do so, are we really doing what the Lord wants us to do?

So I did my homework, and I discovered a number of surprising things about the Bible in relation to the love of God. The first thing I discovered was how very few references to the love of God are to be found in scripture. You can give an impression that the whole Bible is talking about his love but, when you actually get down to studying the matter, you only find thirty-five verses which directly and explicitly refer to the love of God. And do you know how many verses there are in your Bible? Thirty-five thousand! So only one verse in a thousand refers to the love of God. Now that was a big surprise to me. I had thought the Bible was full of it.

The second, even bigger, surprise was that every mention in scripture of the love of God is addressed to those who have already been redeemed by him from slavery — either *slavery in Egypt* under Pharaoh or *slavery to sin* under Satan. Only those who have been rescued by God from slavery talk about the love of God to each other. In the Old Testament, Jews only talked about the love of God to Jews. In the New Testament, Christians only talked about the love of God to Christians. It was an 'in' subject. I believe that the reason for this is that only those who have been redeemed by God can understand his love. Others really do not have enough understanding to grasp what God's love really is until they have been rescued themselves, and redeemed. To take that a little further, note also that neither Jesus nor any of the apostles ever preached about the love of God in public.

Now I always make this appeal to people whom I teach: Do not accept what I say as truth until you have checked me out in your own Bible; see whether I am right or wrong. So in all these things, please check me out, but I could not find a single example of Jesus or the apostles ever preaching about the love of God to unbelievers. The most striking absence is in the Book of Acts, which is surely a description of the early church evangelising, spreading the gospel, planting churches. Yet in the whole of Acts there is not a single mention of the love of God. That is not what they preached. It was not how they spread the gospel. It was not how they planted churches. We have just simply assumed that they did without checking up for ourselves.

So, beginning to add all these data together from

scripture, I came to the conclusion that talking about the love of God to unbelievers is a classic example of something Jesus told us not to do. He said, "Don't throw pearls to pigs". Far from appreciating the value of what you are giving to them, "they will trample them underfoot and turn and rend you to pieces." Now I have never actually preached on that text, and I have never heard a preacher preach on it. But I began to ask: what did Jesus mean? What are the 'pearls' in his mind that he said 'don't throw to pigs' —who will not understand or appreciate? And I have come to the conclusion that talking about the love of God to those who have not been redeemed is precisely an example of 'pearls to pigs'. And Jesus said that if you do that they will turn and attack you. I discovered that when you talk about the love of God to unbelievers they immediately do turn and rend you. At once they come up with two very profound objections: First, how can you then explain the suffering in this world? Second, how can you dare to believe in suffering in the next world? These are the immediate reactions of unbelievers when you tell them God loves everybody.

Natural disasters, especially, become a whip in their hand. The Asian *tsunami* was a classic example. How could a God of love allow things like that, or the earthquake which caused it? How can a loving God sit by and let that kind of thing happen? That is the immediate reaction to our saying that God who made nature and the God who controls nature is a God of love. How can he be?

When it comes to suffering in the next world, the reaction is even stronger. I have written a book entitled *The Road To Hell*. It was wrongly advertised in a national magazine under the heading, 'Read David Pawson's Autobiography'! When the book came out, I was invited more than once to appear on the media to discuss my views. Apparently it is rare today for a preacher to say he still believes in hell. So I would turn up at a BBC studio, and strangely enough they always began with the same question. It became quite boring. The first question of the interview would be: "Now, Mr Pawson, you've written this book on hell. How can a God of love send anyone to hell?" This first question was always the handle to attack me as a Christian. If God is a God of love, how can he send anyone to hell?

I used to reply by asking a question in return. I learned that technique from the Lord himself. I used to say, "Where on earth did you get the idea that God was a God of love?"

Time and time again, I found that this threw the interviewer. "Well . . . well . . . ," they would stammer and stutter, "don't Christians believe that? And didn't Jesus teach that?"

And I used to say, "Well, actually he did. But, you

know, everything I know about hell I have learned from Jesus, because he is the only one in the Bible who talks about it. There's nothing about hell in the Old Testament. Peter doesn't mention it. Paul doesn't mention it. John doesn't mention it. Everything I know about hell came from the lips of Jesus." Now at that point they began to look at the clock and cut the interview a bit short!

As soon as you say to the public 'God loves you', immediately there is the response: why does he allow suffering in this world, and how can you dare to say that he will cause suffering in the next? Put pearls before pigs and they turn and rend you. There are some things that are too precious to be throwing about in public. Another one actually is the fatherhood of God. Do you know that Jesus never talked publicly about the fatherhood of God? He never taught that God is the Father of *everybody*. And fatherhood was so precious to him that in fact it never came into his *public* teaching. Only when he was with his disciples did he talk about 'my Father' and 'your Father'. Fatherhood is very precious. It is a pearl.

* * * * *

In one TV talk that I gave, I happened to say something like this: 'I do not know of a single verse in scripture that tells me clearly that God loves everybody.' We got feedback from that all right! And the feedback invariably said, 'What about John 3:16?' That is why, in this study, we are going to focus on this single verse —because it has been used to justify preaching *a gospel of the love of God*. It has been used as a basis for believing that God loves everybody, without exception. And it has been used in many different ways. This book is not principally about what we should be preaching publicly about God, but, in a word, we should be preaching his *righteousness*.[1] His righteousness is what the Bible majors on. That is what the apostles majored on when they preached. Paul, therefore, was able to say, *I am not ashamed of the gospel, for it is the power of God to save everyone who believes, for in it is revealed a righteousness from God, a righteousness that is from faith to faith, even as it is written, 'the righteous shall live by faith'*. Not a word about the love of God! His gospel was a gospel of righteousness, and that is a good gospel. That is good news. The difference is that when you preach a gospel of righteousness, the very first response you seek is repentance —even before faith. The gospel the apostles preached looked for a response of repentance. You repent towards a God who is righteous.

---

[1] See my companion booklet: *The God and the Gospel of Righteousness*.

2

WHAT'S IN A WORD?

In all that follows, we will concentrate on this single objection which arises when I explain that God's love is not unconditional: 'What about John 3:16?' 'Surely,' so many people say, 'that *is* the gospel of love — about a God who so loved the world that he gave his only-begotten Son; a gospel that calls for believing in him.' But is it? As we look in great depth at this single verse, I want to show that it does not necessarily mean what we thought it meant.

Again, we must remind ourselves that when we really begin to study what the Bible actually does say about the love of God, we find that it is *not unconditional*. We are told that *God loves those who fear him. God loves those who keep his commandments* (see, for example, John 15:10). There are many, many conditions attached to the love of God in the statements we do have. But, as I have pointed out, those statements are all internal to the people of God.

19

Jews talk to each other about the love of God, and so do Christians. We must begin thinking in a new way about scripture. It is regrettable that one French bishop divided the word of God into chapters, and an Irish bishop divided chapters into verses, and we have become 'text people'. The word 'text' originally meant 'everything in a book except the index or the appendix'. 'Text' meant a whole book. It is only in Christian circles that this word has changed to mean one sentence in a book, and that has enabled us to quote a single sentence by itself. We may take it right out of its context and use it in the way that we want to use it. I wish we could get rid of all the chapter and verse numbers.

It has become so convenient. We no longer 'search the scriptures'. We look them up. The damage this has done can easily be demonstrated. Simply ask any group of Christians: 'How many of you can quote John 3:16 to me?' In all likelihood, almost everyone present will confirm that they could do so. Now ask them, 'How many of you could recite John 3:15 for me?' Maybe one or two will indicate they can. Then: 'And now, John 3:17?' A few more, perhaps. Do you see what I mean?

I am going to demonstrate clearly to you that you will not understand John 3:16 without its immediate context, the verses in front of it and behind it, which give it its meaning. Without referring to those verses you will not understand John 3:16. But we have got so used to taking verses by themselves. As we know, the New Testament was originally written in Greek, not our language. And here is an interesting little sidelight: the very first page of a book that has ever been discovered is in the John Rylands library in Manchester. Before the time when it was made, all writing had been on endless scrolls which were rolled up, and it was jolly difficult to take big scrolls around in your pocket! Somebody 'invented' books by cutting the parchment into little squares, sewing them together down one side and writing on both sides. That first page of the first book in history, in Manchester, is a page from John's Gospel. So it may well be the case that the 'book' format was devised to make it more convenient to take the word of God around with you! Now the Greek language was, in one sense, a little more precise than English. By comparison, we tend to be fairly loose with our language. It will be necessary to refer to a little Greek here, simply because the English does not always bring out the clearer meaning of the Greek. Both vocabulary and grammar are involved in this. I do want to underline that I am not trying to make this more complicated than it really is. Far from it. As always, if at any point you think 'I wonder if he is really right about that or not?' – then find someone who knows Greek, (perhaps your pastor) and check me out with them.

Looking at some Greek vocabulary and grammar may seem to be rather pedantic. But you are an adult with a mind; you think, and you want to love God with all your mind, and to be quite sure of your ground.

Turning at last to John 3:16, one of the first things to do is to look at the words that are used, so that you make sure you understand what those words *mean* — that is, what they meant *originally*, when they were written; not just what they mean to you or me, but what they meant to the one who wrote these words and those who read them first. So let us look at the main words used in John 3:16.

'GOD'

The one that sticks out as the great subject of the verse is 'God'. Now most of us do not need to be told what that word means. It means the God of the Bible, the God who made the world, the God from whom we came, the God to whom we go as our Judge, the God of Israel, the God and Father of our Lord Jesus Christ. It is that God we are talking about. It is not any other god. It is not 'Allah', for example. We are talking about the 'God' of the Bible, the Christian 'God'. And we are not talking about the whole Trinity here. We are not talking about Father, Son and Holy Spirit, because the verse is going to refer to the Son separately. God loved and gave his only-begotten Son. So, clearly, 'God' here means God the

Father. That is about all we need to say here concerning this reference to him. It is in this Gospel of John that Jesus is also called 'God' without any qualification. The gospel begins with the statement 'In the beginning was the Word, and the Word was with God, and the Word was God', and it ends with Thomas saying, 'My Lord and my God.' None of the other Gospels applies the word 'God' like that to Jesus, but John does. But here, in John 3:16, John is not talking about Jesus, he is talking about the Father. 'For *God* so loved the world' is a reference to God the Father who gave his Son.

'LOVED'

Next we come to a word that we must consider at greater length: 'loved'. You are probably well aware that in the Greek language there were a number of words that cover our one English word 'love', so we have to pause whenever we see the word 'love' in scripture. We need to ask on each occasion which kind of love is meant, because the English word covers everything from a love of food to a love of anything or anybody. So let me just give you the first little Greek lesson. I am going to highlight three words for love in the Greek language, but there is a fourth which is in a category by itself.

The first Greek word translated 'love' is *epithumia*. That is the lowest kind of love. An equivalent word in English would be 'lust', plain promiscuity. Of course, in the New Testament we learn that this is a 'love' we are to avoid at all costs. It is something purely fleshly. It is dirty. It is not something that God can redeem. It is to be rejected. So although it is one meaning which the word 'love' sometimes expresses in English, we now leave that entirely on one side.

We must concentrate now on the three other common Greek words for love, and I will define them so you can get a real understanding of their meaning. The first is *eros*. You may think, incidentally, there is a statue in Piccadilly Circus, in central London, which bears that name. Wrong! It is popularly called 'Eros' because people think it is a statue of Cupid with a bow and arrow to strike someone's heart. But it is not. The statue ought to be called *Agape* (which I will come to in a moment), because it represents the angel of mercy, not Cupid. It is actually a memorial to Anthony Ashley Cooper, later known as Lord Shaftesbury, who spent a lifetime improving working conditions of the poor in this country and is remembered for that. If you go to Piccadilly Circus, read the inscription on it before you call it Eros. 'Eros' is, essentially, the love of *attraction*. Primarily that would refer to sexual love, which is by far the most common form it takes. Of all the songs ever written, over 75% have been about eros — about attraction between men and women. Understandably so, as it is one of the biggest facts of life, and there is nothing wrong with it. It is not inherently sinful. The mutual attraction between male and female is something God created. So 'eros' is primarily a love of the heart. It is, first and foremost, an involuntary love, something you cannot help, something you cannot turn on and turn off. You fall into it and you fall out of it. It is not so much under your control. Eyes meet across a crowded room, and *eros* takes place. A chemical reaction. A mutual attraction. So that is 'eros'.

God does not 'eros' the world. He is not particularly attracted to us. He has not 'fallen in love' with us. But since the word 'love', in English, is mostly used for *eros*, then it is inappropriate to come with that thought in mind and read John 3:16. It is, in a sense, a selfish love as well, in that it wants to get something from someone else. You are attracted to them. You want to get their attention. You want to get a relationship. You want to get something from the people that you have been attracted to, so that it becomes mutual.

Now the second word is *philia*. From it we get words like 'philadelphia', which means love of brothers. This is the love of *affection*. It is more a love of the mind than the heart. It is finding interests in common. It is, basically, our word 'like'.

So we have *epithumia*, which is our word 'lust'; *eros*,

which is our most common use of the word 'love'; and *phileo*, which is 'like', the love of affection — 'I like him.' 'I like her.' 'We get on together.' 'We have a lot in common.' This is a less selfish love than eros, in that it wants to give as well as to get. It is a two-way business. But it is more a love of the mind: you may have interests in common; you are drawn to each other in affection.

Then we come to the last of the main Greek words translated 'love' —*agape*. This is the love of *action*. In other words, 'eros' is centred in the *heart*, 'phileo' in the *mind* but 'agape' is centred in the *will*. The nearest English word I can get to 'agape' is *care*. To care for someone means giving them two things: your *attention* and your *action*. It is **to do something loving on their behalf**. Essentially, it is a response to someone's need. It is neither a response to their attractiveness nor a response to things which may interest them. To act in *agape* love is to respond to someone else's need, pay attention to that need, and then do something about it.

Between these three different kinds of love there is some overlap, but I have been describing the focus, the centre, of each. One is centred in the heart, one in the mind and one in the will. There will be some emotion attached to *agape* (it is often motivated by feelings of pity and compassion, but there are different Greek words for these), but the essential part of it is in the will, as attention is given to someone in need and something is done about that need. Thus, when somebody came to Jesus and asked about loving one's neighbour, he was told the parable of the Good Samaritan. A man had fallen among thieves and was lying wounded in the road; two people undoubtedly saw him and maybe had feelings for him, but they did not do anything about it, they passed by on the other side. But the Samaritan came by, and he saw this bleeding Jew, his enemy, yet he paid attention, and he took action on his behalf. That is what *agape* love is. It is not to fall in love with someone. It is not to feel affection for someone. It is to pay attention to their condition, and if they are in need to do something about it. Is that not a lovely word?

Because *agape* is centred in the will, it can be commanded. You cannot command people to *eros*. You cannot take a young man and a young woman, put them in a room, and say, 'Thou shalt love one another.' They either fall in love or they don't. You cannot even tell them to *phileo* each other. They might find they have nothing in common. But you can tell them to *agape* each other. Now let us just take this into marriage. When you attend a Christian wedding, invariably 1 Corinthians 13 is read: 'Love is kind. Love suffers long', and all the rest of it. But the word is *agape*. And a Christian marriage is centred in *agape*.

The officiating minister at a wedding does not say, 'Do you like this person . . . ?' He does not say, 'Are you in love with this person?' He says, '*Will* you love her, comfort her, honour, and keep her in sickness and in health ...' —and the response is, 'I will', not, 'I feel like it.' Whatever it turns out like, I will *agape* this person. Now let me make something quite clear – because I have had sad experience of this – a good marriage needs more than *agape*. It must have *eros* in it. I would not marry a couple who did not feel attracted to each other. I would think that pretty fatal. Nor does it depend solely on *phileo*. But I will tell you this: a marriage that only has *eros* won't last. The couple will fall out of love as quickly as they have fallen in. A marriage that has *phileo*, affection, as well, will last longer, but sooner or later a marriage requires *agape* to last a lifetime —a will that is going to give attention and action.

Have I said enough about these words? 'For God so *agape*'d the world . . . .' It does not mean he *liked* the world. It does not mean that he was *attracted* to the world. It does not mean you are attractive to him. It means he **pays attention and does action** when he sees a need.

So when you say to the unbeliever, 'God loves you', what are they going to think? 'Oh, I must be lovable. God must like me. God must be attracted to me. I must be special to God. He must have fallen in love with me.' None of that is included here. But since the world knows very little agape, and a little more phileo, and a whole lot of eros, just simply saying 'God loves you' is going to be misunderstood. It is bound to be, because until you have experienced forgiveness from God you hardly understand what agape can really mean.[1]

That is the word used in John 3:16. So it is not primarily God's attraction to us, nor God's affection for us, but God's attention to our need, and his action on our behalf. 'God so *agape*'d ... that he gave ....' There is the action. That is what he did about what he saw as our need.

'WORLD'

Now we have got to look at the word 'world'. God so loved the world. God the Father *agape*'d it; he paid attention to our need and did something about it. And it was on behalf of the *world*. Now again we've got to look at the meaning of this word in scripture. It is not a geographical word. It is not a reference to our world in the sense of our planet, our globe. 'World' in scripture is always a human word, not geographical. It is a reference to the human race, human society. God so agape'd human society. But I have to say that it's not only a big word, covering the whole human race; it is a *bad* word. The word 'world' in scripture connotes a rather bad image. It is a sinful world. It is a fallen world. It is a rebellious world.

---

[1] *Agape* was little used in the ancient Greek world until Christians filled it with an understanding based on God's revelation in Jesus, for which a new word was needed.

Now John the apostle also wrote letters, and I am going to remind you of something he said in his first letter. *Love not the world. If anyone loves the world, the love of the Father is not in him* (1 John 2:15). Now somehow we have to fit that in with John 3:16. At first sight it seems a straight contradiction: God loved the world, and we are not to. It is alright for him to love it but not for us! It seems to mean that if any Christian, any believer, loves the world, the love of the Father is not in him. What an extraordinary thing to say! And the word is 'agape' in that verse as well. So it's alright for God to agape the world, but it is not alright for us to agape the world. So we're not to copy God in that respect. I'll come back to this later, but for the moment I am pointing out that the word 'world' is a bad word, meaning sinful, fallen, rebellious society. It is not a neutral word. It is that God agape'd a rebellious world that did not love him and did not want to love him.

God has one big problem. I often tell people the Bible is not about *our* problems and God's answers to them. It is about God's answer to *his* problem; and his problem is rebellious kids. That is a well-known problem today! And the Bible is God's solution to God's problem. What do you do with rebellious kids? And 'world' means a whole family of rebellious children. So it is not just that God loves this beautiful world and God loves this human world —it is God loving this rebellious, hating world, and doing something about it.

'BEGOTTEN'

That he gave his only-begotten Son. Let us consider the word *begotten*. Most modern English translations have dropped this word because, again, it is misunderstood and many people have assumed wrongly that the Son of God was not everlasting but that he had a beginning, that he was begotten in the sense that once upon a time there was only God the Father, and then God had a son and 'begat' his son. That is heresy, and the church had to fight for some centuries against it: the idea that the Son of God was not eternal like his Father, but had a beginning at some point in time or eternity, before which he did not exist and after which he did. Today the Jehovah's Witnesses are teaching this, among others. But way back in the early church there was a man called Arius, who taught this, and his views became very popular. A young man called Athanasius had to stand almost alone to say that Jesus was the *eternal* Son of God. The word 'begotten' here is in contradiction, as it were – or at least in contrast – to 'adopted'. There may be a family of adopted children, or another family in which some are adopted and others begotten. Now God has a very big family, but in that family almost all are adopted. They were not begotten by God in the sense of bearing his nature in them, but were brought into his family in another way.

I think the nearest I can get to it in English is to say that Jesus was God's *only natural Son*. I think that gets across the meaning of the word 'begotten'. It does not mean that he had a beginning, but that he was the only one to completely share his Father's nature. By very nature he was God like his Father. The New International Version speaks of God's *one and only* Son, and that is another way of putting it. But I am just trying to explain that it does not mean that Jesus was once begotten, but that he was the *only* begotten, the only one who shared the very nature of the Father, and I hope that clears up an area where misunderstanding can all too easily occur.

When I read that God *so loved the world that he gave his only natural son*, I cannot help thinking of Abraham and Isaac. Isaac was the only 'natural' son Abraham had at that time, Ishmael being illegitimate, and he was willing to offer him up.

'GAVE'

The word 'gave' in verse sixteen is ambiguous. If you take the verse by itself, what does 'gave' mean? How did he give him? Who did he give him to? Why did he give him? It simply says *gave*. Now we know what it means because we know the rest of the story, but it does not say here, for example, whether it refers to giving his son in *birth* or giving him in *death*. We shall see later that it means very clearly giving him in death. But in a sense the Father gave the Son to us when he was born like one of us and became a man. So I just point out that the word 'gave' means a lot to us Christians, but by itself to an unbeliever you would have to explain what the expression 'gave' really meant. Did he give him away to someone else? Or to another father? What does it mean? I am just pointing out that this verse by itself actually needs other verses to enable us to understand it.

'WHOSOEVER'

The word *whosoever* is a regrettable translation because the Greek word is *all*. It does not mean *anyone*, it means *everyone* who believes. It is an inclusive word. It is a wide invitation. It is a whoever so that *everyone who believes in him* —not *so that **anyone** who believes in him*, but *so that **everyone** who believes in him*. It just has a different feel about it. 'Whoever' tends to mean an individual here and there. But it is *so that all*, so that *everyone who believes* . . . . There is a breadth there that does not quite come out in English.

'BELIEVES'

Now look at the word *believes*. It is very important always to notice what word follows the word 'believe'. Here it is the word 'in'. There is a world of difference between believing *that* and believing *in*. I have often asked a congregation the question: 'How many of you believe in me?' A few brave souls raise their hands. Then I ask, 'How many of you believe that I exist?' Everybody responds, indicating that they do. If you word your appeal right, you get a better response! Believing *that* and believing *in* are totally different. I was in a church somewhere overseas where I asked, 'How many of you believe in me?' —and five people put up their hands. I said to one of them, 'Thank you for saying you believe in me, but I don't know if you do or not. You've said you do. You've professed that you do, but I don't know if you really do. Would you give me all your money to look after? I would then know, wouldn't I, that you believe in me?' The whole place went totally quiet. It froze! Afterwards I said to the pastor, 'That didn't go down very well. Why was that?' And he said that she was the richest woman in the town! Her husband had died and left her much real estate in the middle of the city. Reading between the lines, I rather gathered that she had paid for the new church we were in.

It does not say, 'whoever believes *that* Jesus died for their sins . . . .' That is not *believing in*. Believing that Christ died for our sins is *not* saving faith. Believing *in* the Christ who died for your sins is saving faith. Do you see the difference? Believing that God so loved the world that he gave his only-begotten Son is not enough. You can believe all the first part of the verse and believe that it is all true. But still it does not help until you believe *in* him whom he gave. That is a very important point. Just accepting that Christ died for our sins does not save you. Believing in the Christ who died for our sins does. And believing *in* someone means two things: that you **trust** them and that you are willing to **obey** them. Confidence and obedience are both involved in believing in someone. So simply accepting a Christian creed does not do it. Even simply accepting that Christ died for our sins does not do it. But trusting and obeying the Christ who died for your sins does. So that little word *in* is terribly important.

'PERISH'

Now the word *perish*. It sounds a rather weak word, not really strong enough at all. The word 'perish' to me speaks about a hot water bottle that is leaking, or a car tyre that is beginning to give at the tread and the edges —a kind of slow process of disintegration. Is that what the word 'perishing' conveys to you, just something wearing out? Actually, on the contrary, it is a very strong word. It is a word that is usually translated elsewhere as 'destroyed'. And it is a word that means 'destroyed in an act of destruction'. It means *to be ruined*. It means to be rendered useless for the purpose for which something has been made. When a woman came to Jesus one day and poured the precious perfume out on him, the expression was used by Judas Iscariot which meant: That has been ruined; you can never use that again; we will never be able to sell it; it has gone. It is wasted.

'Perish' means to be rendered ruinous, to become a ruin. More than that, the verb means to be ruined, destroyed *by someone*. It is in fact in the middle voice, it is not *shall never perish* but *never be destroyed*. It is the same word as in Matthew 10:28, where Jesus said 'Don't fear those who can kill your body and do nothing more. Fear him who can destroy body and soul in hell.' There is the word again. It is a very powerful word for God ruining someone so that they are utterly useless. It is a terrible word. Again it is not just 'perishing' in the sense of wearing out. 'Perish' means to be ruined, utterly destroyed and made useless for the purpose for which one was made. It does not mean to cease to exist. It means to exist in a state of ruin or utter uselessness. I mention this because there is a new teaching among evangelicals: that hell is the place where you cease to exist. It is called 'annihilation'. Have you come across that idea? If ceasing to exist is what hell is, it is good news to the sinner! To go to sleep after a lifetime of sin, vice and crime and not wake up — that is no punishment at all, is it? It is just oblivion, and people have based it on this word 'destroy'. But to see what it means, think of a castle ruin you may have visited or have seen in a photograph. That helps to provide the right picture for what the word really conveys. If you go to a ruined castle, it is still there. You can see it. It still exists. But it is now totally useless for the purpose for which it was built. The word does not mean to be annihilated, it does mean to be rendered utterly useless. And hell will be packed with people whom God has destroyed, meaning *rendered utterly useless*.[1]

'LIFE'

The word *life* stands out, and of course this is the opposite of death. It is the opposite of 'perish'. It means life which will be totally useful; life that will be fulfilling for the purpose for which it was made; life that will be totally satisfying. So the contrast is with perishing —when you do not cease to be, but you go on being utterly useless. You can go on being totally useful. That is satisfying.

---

[1] See my book *The Road to Hell* (Terra Nova Publications).

'ETERNAL'

Scholars debate the word 'eternal' which is used here. Some think it is a word of *quantity*, and others a word of *quality*. When you think of quantity it is translated *everlasting* —life that goes on forever. But others say that eternal life means life of a good quality; it is life worth living. The whole debate about euthanasia is as to whether life is worth living. So does *eternal* mean 'worth living' as well? I think the answer is *both* quantity and quality of life. It means both everlasting and abundant. The word has got it all wrapped up. It will be life that goes on forever. (But, frankly, life for some people going on forever would be hell.) 'Eternal' life means life of a quality that makes every moment worthwhile.

* * * * *

We have looked at some of the actual words of John 3:16, and now we must move on to its grammar. This is where we get into real detail and where we are going to make some very startling discoveries. I did not like English grammar at school, but now I really value it because it helps you to understand how words are put together: which words have the major emphasis; what the sentence is saying; what the main clause is, and what the subsidiary clause is. It helps you to take a sentence to pieces and look at how it is put together. That is very important.

The particular aspect of grammar that I want to mention which is crucial to understanding this verse is what I call *verb tenses*. Tenses of verbs are very important. For example, we tend to work with three simple tenses of verbs — past, present and future. I *did* talk to my wife before I began writing today; I *am* writing now; and I *will* probably be talking to her again when I have finished putting pen to paper. I have just used a past and a present and a future tense, and you understood exactly what I meant: past tense for something I *did* in the past; present tense for what I am *doing* now, and future tense for what I will probably *be doing* in the future. The Greek language, too, has past, present and future tenses, but it also has rather finer distinctions than we have between those tenses. The particular one I must introduce you to is this (and I will try to be as simple and straightforward as I can here): some 'past' verbs in Greek refer to something that happened only once, and other tenses refer to something that happened repeatedly, continuously.

In English we do not have that fine distinction. For example, our past tenses usually end in *–ed* [the verb], but when you have a verb ending *–ed* it does not tell you whether it happened once or many times. For example, if I say to you that the new ship called the QM2 sailed from Southampton, which of these do you think I meant — that it did it once or regularly? One has no idea. 'Sailed' past tense does not tell you whether I am referring to her *once* sailing from Southampton or, alternatively, suggesting that Southampton was her home base, and that she regularly sailed from there.

Or if I said, 'I had porridge for breakfast', again it would be unclear whether I did so once or regularly. The Greek would tell you straightaway in each example whether it meant once or many times. When the Greeks talked about something in the past they had one tense that meant it happened regularly and another tense which signified that it happened only once. Now which tense do you think is used for 'crucified'? Christ crucified — once, because it only ever happened once. The tense that expresses this is called the *aorist* tense, and when you find the aorist tense you know that it happened once.

Now the other tense I want to introduce you to is the present tense, but in Greek it is called the *present continuous tense*. It means something that you are doing and will go on doing continuously. Now this opens up many scriptures in a new light. For example, Jesus did not say, 'Ask and you will receive, seek and you will find, knock and it will be open to you.' The verbs there are all present continuous tense, and we have to add the words 'go on' in English to bring out that meaning. 'Jesus said, "Go on asking and you will receive. Go on seeking and you will find. Go on knocking and the door will open to you."' — Not just do it once, but go on doing it. Even at the end of John's Gospel, Jesus appears to Mary in the garden outside the tomb after his resurrection. In English it says, 'Jesus said to her, "Touch me not."' But actually the word 'touch' is in the present continuous tense, and therefore what Jesus really said was, "Don't go on touching me." Now when you read 'Touch me not', I have heard preachers say that you could not get hold of his resurrection body and he was forbidding her to touch it. Not so, he was saying, 'Stop touching me. Do not hang onto me, because I am going to my Father.'

Now I begin to look at the verbs used in John 3:16. First of all, guess which tense the word *gave* is in. The answer is aorist. God only *gave* his Son once, he did not *go on* giving him. He just gave him once, on one occasion. What an important occasion that was, nevertheless. I just want to point out that it doesn't say 'God goes on giving . . . .' He *once* gave his Son — only once. The word 'perish' is also in that same aorist tense. It happens only once. A person is only destroyed once and it is permanent; they are ruined once.

By the way, that does mean that John 3:16 is talking about God destroying people, so we must understand 'loved the world' in the light of this. This is the same God who destroys, who causes them to perish.

There are, then, two aorists which many people

interpret as present continuous. God does not *go on* giving and he does not *go on* destroying, he does each of them once only.

But now let us look at two continuous verbs. The first, and one of the most important, is *believes*. It ends in English with *–es*, not with *–ed*. It is not *whoever once believed*, but whoever *goes on believing* . . . and this is characteristic of John's Gospel. When he uses the word *believe*, he puts it in the present continuous tense as something you *go on* doing. One step of faith does not save a person. ***Going on believing will save them***. Faith is a continuing thing, so you cannot say, 'Well, I once believed, therefore I'm saved.' No, you *go on* believing. 'Whoever goes on believing in him . . . . ' Faith is a continuing relationship of confidence and obedience. If you stop believing, then you stop being a believer, and you can fall into unbelief. Paul talks about that in Romans chapter 11 quite a lot. He said that some of the Jews were cut off, and, ' . . . you too will be cut off if you do not continue in God's kindness.' It is not the faith you had twenty years ago that will save you, it is the faith you have at the end; not the faith that starts, but the faith that finishes.

This is a very fundamental teaching and insight into the meaning of *believing* in scripture. It is usually in the present continuous tense, that *'whoever goes on believing in him'*, and the *–es*, even in the English, should tell you that. It is not *'whoever believed'* (in the past), it is *'whoever is believing'* (in the present), whoever *believes*. Imagine if you were to see a road accident, and there is a body lying there next to an overturned motorbike. You go up to the scene and somebody says to you, 'He breath*es* . . . .' You would assume that he is *continuously* breathing. 'He is breathing', present continuous. If they said, 'He breath*ed* . . .' with a 'd' at the end of the word, you would assume he was dead, that he has stopped breathing; but if they say (present tense), 'He breathes' (he *is* breathing), then you know it is continuous.

Now, the next verb which is a surprise is *have*. *Whoever believes* [or, *everybody who believes in him, who goes on believing in him*], *will go on having eternal life*. Now does that change the meaning of this verse for you a little? It does for me. It is those who *go on* believing, who *go on having life*. Those who do not go on believing will not go on having life. I will come back to this later, but that is essential to an understanding of John 3:16. Those who go on believing will go on having life, therefore those who do not go on believing will lose life. That is a very important point. So eternal life can be lost. How can such a thing happen? We will return to this point.

Now we come to the biggest surprise of all, and the one that will alter the meaning for you more than any other point. Guess which tense the verb 'love' is in. Is it *'once*, on one occasion', or is it continuously? The answer is, *For God so loved the world* is in the aorist tense. If you know the tenses of Greek verbs you will be able to check me out. The aorist tense means that on one occasion God *once* loved the world. Now, how many people reading John 3:16 immediately change that verb 'loved' to 'loves' in their minds? They immediately think of a continuous relationship between God and the world that goes on and on. I have even heard preachers quote it and say '. . . for God so loves the world', as if it is present continuous tense. It is not. It is saying that on one occasion, once in history, God *agape*'d the world. Bear in mind that agape means *acting to meet a need*, then you can understand why the word 'loved' is not in the present continuous tense. But most people come to John 3:16 and say, 'There, that is biblical proof that God loves everybody all the time.' But it does not say that. It tells us that he once, on one occasion, acted on behalf of our rebellious, sinful race – and praise God that he did. But do you see what I am saying? We cannot build on this verse the idea that God loves everybody or that he loves us all the time or what people imply when they speak of 'unconditional love of God'. It is not there in the text.

That really is a big surprise. If we are not careful, we tend to reverse the tenses of the verbs and read *loved* as meaning 'all the time' and *believed* as meaning 'once'. The way it is preached is almost: 'God's love is there all the time; all you need do is, in a moment, take a simple step of faith — and you've got eternal life.' But it is not that at all. That is reversing the verbs. 'God [once] loved so that whoever [continuously] believes . . . will never perish [once], but have [continuously] eternal life.' This also explains the apparent contradiction in 1 John 2:15, where it says 'Love not the world. If anyone loves the world, the love of the Father is not in him.' The word 'love' there is agape, but it is in the present continuous tense. It is for those who go on paying attention to the world and getting involved in it, so the contrast is between John 3:16, where God once loved the world, and John's letter, where he says: Do not go on [continuously] loving the world. God did not even go on [continuously] loving the world, he *once* loved and did everything that was needed to meet the world's need. That focuses his love down to a single event, and that is why Paul, in Romans, writing to Christians, says, 'God commends his love towards us, in that while we were still sinners, Christ died for us' (Romans 5:8).

God's love is not general and unfocused; it is not vague and all over the place. God's love is always focused. It is focused in the cross of Jesus, and it is focused in him paying attention to our need and then doing something radical about that need.

3

THE GOD WHO KILLS

You may feel that, having given so much attention to John 3:16, we have now covered it adequately, but we haven't. There is much more that needs to be said. Thus far we have neglected the two smallest words in the verse, and they are going to prove to be the most important – one is a word of three letters, and one of two letters. The three-letter word is *for*. Did you ever notice that word? '*For* . . . *God so loved the world*. Why is it there? There must be a reason for it.

We shall also see that the most important (and most misunderstood) word is the two-letter word *so*.

'FOR'

The first word to consider is *for*. What is that word there for? What does it mean when you begin a sentence with 'For'? Perhaps you have never asked that question. Most people don't even notice. 'For' is usually a word that creates a link with the previous sentence. 'For' indicates that you are going to expand on something, or explain something, or take it a step further, which means that verse 16 cannot make sense without verse 15 and verse 14, because 14 and 15 are one sentence. Verse 16 does not just begin, 'God so loved the world that he gave', it is: 'For . . . God so loved the world'. So we need to ask what is being expanded or explained.

'SO'

When we come to that most misleading and mis-understood word 'so', quite frankly the English translations put the word *so* in the wrong place. In the Greek it comes right at the beginning of the sentence, and in the Greek language the first word in a sentence is the one that is being emphasised as most important. Literally, the Greek says, *So for God loved the world*. So what does *so* mean?

Regrettably, English readers always put a mental extra word in after the word *so*. God loved the world so *much* or so *deeply* . . . that he gave his only-begotten Son. That is not what the word means at all. Even the Amplified Version of scripture got it wrong. It says, 'For God so greatly loved and dearly prized the world' (AMP), and again that is what the mind tends to do in reading the word *so* coming after the word *God*, but it should come before. *For so . . . God loved the world . . . .* The word 'so' does not mean 'so much', 'so greatly' or 'so deeply'. In fact, the Greek word actually means 'thus' or 'in this way', or 'in just the same way'. *He did it just so.* Now do you understand the meaning of it? *He did it in this way. This is how he did it.* In fact, the literal meaning of the word is 'thus'. 'For thus' [God loved the world]; 'For in this way' [God loved the world]; 'For in the same way as this' [God loved the world]. Are you getting the feel of it? It is *not* 'for so much' or 'so deeply' or 'so greatly' [God loved the world]. You tend to read the word *so* as if it had three syllables: God *so-o-o* loved the world . . . . And that is how most people take it, but it isn't that; it is, 'Thus'; 'In this way'; 'So' God loved the world; 'So . . .' (this is how he did it).

Now that really alters the whole thing. We could translate it 'Just so' or 'Even so', and if you cast your eyes back to the previous sentence, 'As Moses lifted up the serpent in the wilderness, even so . . . ', (there is the word again), 'even so, the Son of man must be lifted up.' 'Even thus.' 'Even in this way.' 'Even in the same way.' It is the same word in the previous sentence, so it could be translated in verse 16, 'For even so, God loved the world.'

It is not a quantity word at all, it is a comparison word:

'That this happened and, even so, in the same way, this also happened.'

All this means that the words 'for' and 'so' both link verse 16 with what has gone before. That is why I say you cannot understand verse 16 by itself. 'For, in this way'; 'For, in the same way . . . .' We can translate the word 'for' by the word 'indeed'. That is another link word that means you are going to expand on something or explain it. 'Indeed, in the same way, God loved the world . . . .' In the same way as what? Well, in the same way as has just been mentioned. So here is the classic case of a text needing its context. 'God loved the world in the same way . . .' [as a previous occasion on which he did something]. In other words, verse 16 is the second occasion on which God did something loving. So what was the first? So both *for* and *so* refer to the context.

Before we go any further, let me translate verse 16 in the light of what we have discovered so far. I would say something like this:

Indeed, in just the same way, God the Father acted in love on another occasion, this time for the whole rebellious human race, by sacrificing his only natural Son so that all who go on trusting and obeying him might never be ruined beyond recovery, but go on having everlasting and abundant life.

That is a paraphrase rather than a literal translation, but it communicates what we have already seen in the verse.

Now let us go beyond the verse itself and explore the

context. What was the earlier occasion on which God did something similar? We have to ask this because it is a verse that begins, 'Indeed, in just the same way, God acted in love, in just the same way as a previous occasion' – and verses 14 and 15 tell you how God did a loving thing on a previous occasion, in much the same way. Verses 14 and 15, as I have explained, are one sentence; they should not be divided into two verses. This tells about something that you can read about more fully in Numbers 21.

Let us just paint the scene for a moment. There are six hundred thousand men, to say nothing of the women and children – just over two million people – stuck in a desert without food or water, and they are there through their own fault entirely. They are the children of Israel in the wilderness of Sinai. What has happened is this: they have met with God at Mount Sinai; God has conducted a marriage service with them; they have said 'I will', and he has said 'I will', and they have been married, as God and Israel together. God has given them his commandments – how he wants them to live – and then he has said: Now go and possess the Promised Land that I am giving you. We are told that it is less than ten days from Sinai into the Promised Land. They could have been there in less than a fortnight, but when they arrived at a place called Kadesh Barnea they got cold feet. They said, 'We'd better send spies in to find out about this Promised Land before we go in.' And they chose twelve men, one from each tribe. They went in, and they came back with the most luscious grapes. And they said, 'It's flowing with milk and honey, it's a wonderful land, but the city walls are sky high and the people are much bigger than we are; they are giants in there and we'll never take it. No way.' Of the twelve spies who went in, ten said that, but two said, 'Let's go in.'

God said, 'I will take you in, and I will carry you on my shoulders so that you will be bigger than the giants.' They still did not believe it. Of course, they had not as yet seen Jericho's walls fall down. They took a vote on it and they said, 'We are staying here, we are not going in.' The result was that for forty years they wandered in the desert – for a whole generation – and the only two who got into the Promised Land were the two spies who said 'we can go in.'

So there they were, stuck in the desert for forty years, with no food and no water. But God decided to have mercy on them, and he gave them food every day, enough vitamins, minerals, carbohydrates and proteins, all dressed up in little round beads of food which dropped every morning on the desert floor. Twice as much dropped every Friday so they did not have to go out and get it the next day. (That proves it was a miracle because none of the scientific explanations allow for the double dose on Fridays!) Anyway, they called it *'What is it?'* —in Hebrew, *manna*. They had 'What is it?' for breakfast, 'What is it?' for lunch, 'What is it?' for supper. The children might have said, "'What is it' for lunch, mummy?"

"Yes! 'What is it' for supper, too!"

It was adequate food to keep them healthy and fit, but they began to grumble. They were fed up with this 'What is it?', and they began to wish they were back in slavery in Egypt, because there they had garlic and spices. They had had interesting food, and they grumbled at the food God was giving them, even though it was keeping them alive and they should not have needed it because they should have gone into the Promised Land when he told them. It is entirely their own fault, yet God has pity on them and feeds them. But they grumble. They went to Moses and said, 'We are fed up with this food. Why did you bring us out of Egypt? And you can tell God, too, we're fed up.'

God was angry with them because of the sin of in-gratitude. He was feeding them and giving them water from the rock. Even though they were there for their own fault and their own stubborn lack of faith in God, he was still keeping them alive, and here they were, grumbling. So he sent venomous snakes among them and many people died. These snakes were so venomous and so numerous that the survivors began to put two and two together. They said, 'This isn't a natural disaster, this is God. He's killing us off for ingratitude', and they confessed it to Moses. They went to him and said, 'Moses, we have sinned and we know it. We've sinned against you, we've sinned against God. Please ask him to remove the snakes.'

The important point in the story is this: *God refused to take the snakes away*. He said, 'No, the snakes stay, and they will go on biting people, and people will go on dying. What I will do, however, is give them a way of escape from death. I won't take the snakes away, but Moses, I want you to do this: make a bronze snake and attach it to a big pole, a stake, and go to the nearest hill overlooking the camp, and put the stake with the snake on it up on top of that hill. And then tell the people: When you are bitten, if you go and look at that snake the venom will not be fatal.'

This is a very important point. God did not take the snakes away. The people were still under constant threat of death, but he gave them a way of escape. It says that when anybody was bitten, if they went up to the hill and gazed at this metal snake, the venom would lose its power to kill and they would be healed. Now *that* is the story of the first occasion when God loved. **And it was in just the same way that God loved the rebellious world and gave his Son**. Here is a parallel which is drawn by Jesus himself: 'As Moses lifted up the serpent, so must the Son of Man be lifted up.' Now then, what do we deduce from this amazing link between John 3:16 and that sordid event in Israel's history? Well the first thing that I would draw from that is this, and it is most important: the God of Israel is the God and Father of Jesus; the same God, the God of the Old Testament, is the God of the New Testament, and *vice versa*. Why do I make that point? Because there is a heresy, hundreds of years old, which has now re-emerged among evangelicals today in our twenty-first century, and the heresy was named after the first man who taught it. His name was Marcion, and the heresy to this day is called Marcionism.

The heresy is quite simple: namely the claim that the God of the Old Testament and the God of the New Testament are not one and the same God. Marcion's view was: 'I don't like the God of the Old Testament at all; he's a harsh God; he kills people off; I believe in the God of the New Testament, the loving Father of Jesus' —and it has been common ever since for people to set over against each other the picture of God in the Old Testament and the picture of God in the New. Have you ever come across it? I think you have, actually. It is becoming very common today to talk about the God of the Old Testament as a kind of harsh, destroying God, the sort of God you would not like, in contrast with this 'nice' God of the New Testament who is kind and patient and loving, as if they are two quite different kinds of God.

It is coming back today in all its force with this huge emphasis on the loving God. People are playing down the revelation of God in the Old Testament, and I am going to mention two writers who are being listened to today. The most popular, widely read author in the Christian world today is Philip Yancey. I was recently asked to recommend his latest book, but when I read it I said I could not possibly do so because in it he quoted with approval the statement that Jesus came to show us the 'mother love' of God, as distinct from the 'father love' of God in the Old Testament. Now there it is in a rather subtle form, but it is the same idea: that the God of the Old Testament is somehow a bit hard and a disciplinarian, whereas the God of the New Testament is more like your mum. That is heresy. It goes against John 3:16, because it is against John 3:14–15.

Huge controversy has also arisen about a book by Steve Chalke, who is one of the most prominent evangelical communicators in the world today. Mainly, people have found what he has said about the cross very offensive (that if Jesus was punished for sins he had not committed, that was a case of 'cosmic child abuse'). My problem with the book is not just what he says about the cross, but that his over-emphasis on the love of God appears to suggest to the reader that the God of the Old Testament was 'guilty of ethnic cleansing' when he ordered the Canaanites to be slaughtered, as if the God who ordered that is somehow a different God from the God of the New Testament whom we learn about in Jesus.

But here, in John chapter 3, the God who killed Israelites off for grumbling about the food is the God who loved the world and gave his only Son. Same God! And his loving act towards Israel was not to remove the snakes, but to give people a way to escape; and in the same way, he has done the same for us by giving his Son. And his Son is now our 'snake on the stake'.

Do you understand what we are saying? Here in John's Gospel, the God of the Old Testament who puts people to death for ingratitude, is the same God who gives his only Son to us. There is no wedge here between the God of the Old Testament and the God of the New. This is very important. But when you take verse 16 by itself, and ignore verses 14 and 15, you may well be misled into thinking that the God of the New Testament is not the God of the Old, and that he is much kinder and more loving than he was then, whereas John is saying, 'In the same way'; 'Just so'.

Just so. The same God who gave them a way out of death. Our world is under sentence of death, as they were, and God is not removing that sentence of death. *What he is doing is giving us a way to escape death*. Now that to me is very, very important. The God of John 3:16 is the God of 3:15 and 3:14, and he is the God of Numbers 21, and the God who dealt with his people in that way then will deal with his people in the same way today. There must never be a wedge driven in between the God of the Old and the God of the New Testament.

When God did that loving act towards the children of Israel, in spite of their rebellion, their lack of faith, their ingratitude – in spite of that – when he still showed by loving action and giving them a way of escape, when all that was the case, then why did God tell Moses to make a metal snake and put it up on a pole? It seems almost an irrelevant or strange thing to do, but it tells us, when you think about it, God already knew about the second loving act he would make. God already knew he was going to have to hang his own Son up on a stake of wood, and was deliberately giving Moses and the children of Israel a picture of what he was going to do, so that when it actually happened they could link it up in their minds, and it would help them to understand what was going on.

The importance to our understanding of John 3:16 of that account in Numbers 21 cannot be overstated. When you read John 3:16 you must have in mind that previous event, when God destroyed so many of his own people for the sin of ingratitude, and he did not take away the threat of death, he simply – in love – gave them a way of escape. *That is the love of John 3:16 as well.* It is saying: *In the similar way, this ungrateful, rebellious world is under sentence of death from God, but God once acted in love and provided a way out and into eternal life.*

Once again, you see, to build a huge doctrine of God loving *everybody* on verse 16 is ignoring all that. And he is a God who has the whole world under sentence of death, even now. When you read Romans chapter 1, one of the sins Paul singles out – one of the worst sins in the world – is: they don't thank God. For that sin alone, our world deserves to die. Living without thanking God.

I can remember the testimony of a top pilot of a major airline who was soundly converted. When he gave his testimony, he said: 'I had so much. I had my health, I had the best job in the world that I wanted, I had a beautiful home and a beautiful family, I had everything a man could want except one thing.' People waited, and he said: 'I had no-one to thank.' No-one to thank. I believe that is a picture of our whole world —not thanking God. Grumbling like mad when a tsunami comes; blaming God for troubles in the world; and then, when things are right, saying thank you? No, ignoring him. God would be justified in sending venomous snakes all over us, too. Are you getting the feel of this verse? The God who was killing Israelites off with snakes, in an act of love, gave them a way out. *In just the same way* God has given this world a way out *when he once loved and once gave his Son.* **This is not a verse about God loving everybody. It is a verse about God providing a way out.** Praise God for that!

4

TEACHER IN THE DARK

Remember that Jesus is talking to Nicodemus, an Old Testament scholar, and he is telling him that what Moses did to that snake will one day happen to himself, and he would be stuck up on a pole, on a hill, for all to see. Nicodemus was already an old man. Do we know if he lived to see that? Yes we do. Though you may not have noticed it, when Jesus was actually nailed to the cross and strung up like that snake on a stake, Nicodemus saw it. They took Jesus' body down. The body of a criminal crucified was normally thrown into the Valley of Gehenna, south of Jerusalem, with all the rubbish and the sewage, outside the 'dung gate' on the south side, and they would have thrown Jesus' body there, but Joseph of Arimathea came, and he said, 'He can have my tomb.' Nicodemus said, 'I'll help you bury him.' So it was that three years after hearing Jesus' words, Nicodemus is taking the body of Jesus down from the stake and laying it in the tomb. He and Joseph did it together. Had you noticed that? You see, Nicodemus knew the Old Testament backwards. He knew all about this story of the snake in the wilderness, and here is Jesus using that Old Testament picture, which means that God already had it all in his mind – what he was going to do to his son Jesus – and was giving the children of Israel a picture to remember. The tragedy is, of course, that the snake on a pole was kept for years after the event. They took it with them into the Promised Land; they set it up as an idol in that land, and they burned incense to it and prayed to it, this snake on a stick, until finally one of the good kings of Israel said, 'I'm putting a stop to that', and he took the snake and the pole and smashed it to smithereens, telling the people they were no longer going to venerate that symbol because its day was done.

John chapter 3 is about a private conversation with Nicodemus, and again, if we are going to approach verse 16 in the right way, we need to go through this conversation, because that is where it all came up. Three of the Gospels are about the public discourses of Jesus, but in John's, which is very intimate, there are a good many private conversations: with Nathanael, the woman at the well, and here Nicodemus. He came by night. But why? Out of sheer self-protection. He is called '*the* teacher in Israel', not *a* teacher in Israel. He was the man who was the top theologian in the nation, the one who was supposed to have answers for everybody else, the one thought to be the wisest man. He was coming by night because he did not want it known publicly that he had a lot to learn himself. He was humble enough to know that, and to come to Jesus and ask questions, but it is understandable that he did not want to do so publicly. The reputation of the teacher in Israel, the man with all the answers, was at stake, yet, deep in his heart, he had questions.

Why, then, did he come? Because he was a secret admirer of Jesus. There was something in Jesus' ministry that he had never known, that he wanted, that he envied, admired, and coveted. There was a dimension to Jesus' teaching that was missing in his own, even though he had the reputation of being the top teacher of the whole nation. This combination of humility and yet protecting his reputation on the other hand is very interesting: Jesus, you are a better teacher than I am. There is something about your teaching that I don't have.

The two things Nicodemus highlighted were authority and power. We are told that, when Jesus taught, the common people heard him gladly because *he spoke with authority*. The common people could say about Jesus, 'This man knows what he's talking about.' 'Common people' are usually pretty good judges of character and of teachers, and they vote with their feet quite readily.

They were listening to a man who knew what he was talking about. Sophisticated people can often be fooled quite easily. Clever people are the easiest people to fool. Dress it up in the right language, and they fall for it, but it is much harder to fool common people. Common people say that the emperor has no clothes, and they walk away. Common people heard Jesus gladly because he spoke with authority. He knew what he was talking about. *He also taught with power.* When he said to a demoniac, 'Get out . . .', the demons went. When he said, 'Be healed,' people were healed. These were the two things in Jesus' teaching that Nicodemus did not have. Oh, he had plenty of theology. He had learned, he was a good teacher. I call it 'emptying the church by degrees!' Nicodemus came, and said, in effect: God is with you. I have come to the conclusion that when you teach, God is with your teaching. What an admission! He was really saying: God is not with me . . . and yet I'm the teacher in Israel, but I need what you've got. He is really saying: How can I be like you? But of course scholars never ask personal questions, they always put it in the third person. 'How can a man . . . ?' 'How can this happen?' Nicodemus would not have said, 'How can I?' But that was the question in his heart – 'How can I be a teacher like you?'

It is not surprising that Jesus should talk then about the kingdom of God, which means the rule of God, the power of God, the authority of God. Most of Jesus' teaching was about the kingdom of God, and quite clearly Nicodemus did not teach the kingdom of God. He couldn't. So Jesus began by talking to him about the kingdom, but he very quickly went on to the power of the Holy Spirit, because that was the missing dimension in Nicodemus' teaching. Nicodemus was a stranger to the kingdom, a stranger to the Holy Spirit, so Jesus then talked to him very simply: 'Nicodemus, you are going to have to start all over again. You're going to have to be born again.'

Now Nicodemus was not a fool, he was a sophisticated scholar, and although he said, 'How can I enter into my mother's womb again and be born?' (I know that's a silly question, isn't it?), he is not really being silly. He is asking in a scholarly way: I am too old to start again. How can a man be born again when he is old? This man is old, and Jesus is saying: Well, my advice to you is start all over again; begin again; be born again. Do not read more into Jesus' words than is there. He is saying: Go right back to the start; start life all over again.

Nicodemus is really asking: How can I do that? I am too old. You cannot put me back in my mother's tummy and start all over again. I'm too old to change. How can I, when I'm old? So Jesus went on to say: 'You need to start again out of water and Spirit.' Quite literally, for again our translations do not bring out the word. In the Greek it is: '. . . except a man be born *out of* water and

Spirit, he cannot even see the kingdom of God.'

There is so much discussion as to what is meant by 'water' there. What did Jesus mean by this? A common evangelical interpretation is that Jesus is referring to two births: *a birth out of water*, your physical birth, and *a birth out of Spirit*, your spiritual birth. I do not think for one moment that is what Jesus meant. It would be a bit redundant to say a man must be born physically as well as spiritually. How could it be otherwise? Some people want to get around 'water' by saying it is the bag of waters that burst just before a baby comes into the world — that is 'born of water', and then, later, they are 'born of Spirit' when they are converted. I do not believe that is the meaning — that it refers to two births. I do believe that it refers to two baptisms: a baptism in water and a baptism in Spirit. The word 'out' there is very important, out of, [*ex*, from which we get the word 'exit'] —born again out of water and Spirit. You cannot come out of something until you have been put into it. But I believe, quite simply, that Jesus is telling Nicodemus how he began his ministry, not just how Nicodemus could.

We often forget that for thirty years Jesus could not do a single miracle. In some of the 'apocryphal gospels' as they are called (which are not in your Bible – like the gospel of Thomas and the gospel of Philip, which are legendary and made up years later), Jesus does miracles when he is a boy. On one occasion, it was said, a boy pushed Jesus over into the mud so Jesus cursed him with leprosy. Aren't you glad that isn't in your Bible? On another occasion, Jesus fashions birds out of clay, blesses them and they fly away. Aren't you glad that's not in your Bible, too? They are in those bad 'gospels', but they're not in our Bible. You see, the truth is that until he was thirty Jesus could make chairs and tables but did not have a ministry. He could not do any miracles —because he did not do his miracles by virtue of the fact that he was the Son of God, but because he was the Son of Man filled with the Holy Spirit. Later he was to say, 'If I cast out demons by the Spirit of God, then the kingdom of God has come upon you.' He acknowledged that his power and his authority belonged to the Holy Spirit. And how did he begin his ministry? Out of water and Spirit. Luke's Gospel tells us that as Jesus came up out of the water from the river Jordan and was praying, the heavens opened and the Holy Spirit descended on him like a dove. That was when Jesus began his powerful ministry, not before. No wonder the people of Nazareth said, 'Isn't this the carpenter's son? Yet we never saw him do things like this at home.'

Jesus began his ministry when he came up out of water and the Spirit flooded him —and he is now saying to Nicodemus, 'You'll have to begin all over again.' He is almost saying: I began my work at the age of thirty out of water and Spirit. From then on, Jesus had a powerful ministry with authority and power over sickness and demons and everything else. He is answering Nicodemus's question. So often, again, we take a verse out of context and say, 'Unless a man is born again out of water and Spirit [or 'of water and Spirit'], he cannot see the kingdom of God', but this was said to Nicodemus, who has asked: How can I have a ministry like yours? And Jesus is giving him the answer: 'Water and Spirit'. Nicodemus, the chief teacher in Israel, would not have been baptised by John the Baptist. The Pharisees would not be baptised by John. Water and Spirit, I believe, refers to two baptisms, and it means, too, that ordinary people like you and me can also exercise a powerful ministry —if we begin again with the two baptisms: water and Spirit.

On the last night of his life on earth, Jesus said, 'The works that I do, you can do, you will do, when power has come upon you . . .' and it did! That is my understanding. I believe Jesus is saying: Nicodemus, this is how it began for me at the age of thirty. It can begin for you in the same way, and it can begin for anybody else in the same way.

So Jesus has really answered Nicodemus's first implicit question: How can I, old as I am, start again like you? It was gloriously possible. But he went on. It was not only, 'How can a man do this?' but he was really asking, How can I? Jesus said that what is born of the flesh is of the flesh, and what is born of the Spirit is of the Spirit. And you cannot manipulate the Spirit. Like the wind, you cannot control the Holy Spirit. You cannot say where the wind came from or where it is going to, but you know when it has hit you. The one thing you do know about the wind is when you feel it, and when it impacts you. Jesus said that it is like that with the Spirit; you cannot explain where the Spirit is coming from or where he is going to, but you will know when he has reached you, and that is all you need to know.

Then Jesus said, 'How is it you, the teacher in Israel, don't even know anything about all this? How can you be claiming to teach everybody else in the nation, and you need to be told these simple things? And I,' he said, 'I am telling you about earthly things; if I talked to you about heavenly things, if you cannot even understand the earthly things I am saying, how on earth will you ever understand heavenly things?' Jesus is challenging Nicodemus here because this man is the professed theologian for the nation, we might say 'the Archbishop of Israel'! 'You need to be taught these simple things,' says Jesus. 'You see, nobody has been up to heaven, so how can we know heavenly things? Well, the answer is somebody has come down from heaven to tell us —and I am talking to you now. The Son of Man. And I have brought heavenly truths for you.' What a claim!

Nicodemus then asks his third question. Question number one was: How can I be a teacher like you?

Question number two was: How can an old man start all over again? Question number three: How can this happen? Do you notice, he never says, 'How can it happen to me?' or, 'How can I be born again?' He always says, 'How can a man be born again?' 'How can such things be?' 'How can such a thing happen to anyone?' He is really asking: How can I have the Holy Spirit? How can he come to me?

It is now that Jesus introduces the Moses' serpent episode. Why? Try to think of the connection. The answer is really very simple. **You cannot have the Holy Spirit impact your ministry until you have believed in Jesus. The cross must be understood first.** It is as simple as that. It is people who have come to the cross, and believed in him who died there, who are now eligible to receive the wind of the Spirit. So Jesus is again answering Nicodemus's question, and he is saying, 'I will have to explain something else to you now — not only that the Son of Man came down from heaven, but that the Son of Man must be lifted up on a stake, just as Moses lifted the serpent up.'

Can you see how Jesus is leading this man, step by step, to an understanding of what will transform him as a person, and transform his ministry? —by going to the cross, believing in him who died there, and then receiving the power of the Holy Spirit into his life. It is really quite a discussion. Of course, it went on for hours and we only have a bit of the discussion, but I have given you the gist of it. Can you see how it is flowing?

Now we are ready to look at John 3:16 again. Jesus is answering Nicodemus's questions one by one, but we haven't exhausted 3:16 yet. We now need to ask a most important question. I have what is called a 'red letter Bible', in which Jesus' words are printed in red and the rest is in black print. Where does the red print end? If I look at the quotation marks that indicate what Nicodemus said to Jesus and what Jesus said to Nicodemus, they open again in verse 10. Where do they end after verse 10? The point is that we need to know who said verse 16. Most people think that Jesus said it to Nicodemus. Now Jesus certainly said verses 14 and 15, but did he say verse 16? That is the question. When any verse of the Bible is under study, you ask: Who said this, and to whom did they say it, and why did they say it? Well I want to tell you that I am totally convinced that Jesus did not say verse 16 to Nicodemus. And that is a very important point. In the New International Version the quotation marks do not end until verse 21, but at the foot of the page it says that some interpreters end the quotation marks at verse 15. Have you got that little note in your Bible? Well, you can cross out whatever it says and put the quotation marks back at the end of verse 15, because that is when the conversation with Nicodemus ended.

I want to give you five reasons why I believe that. Verse 22, of course, turns to narrative. After this, Jesus and his disciples went into the Judean countryside and so on, so that is clearly not the conversation, but I want to say the conversation ended at verse 15, so here are the five reasons. First of all, there is unnecessary repetition at the end of verse 15 and verse 16. Have you noticed that funny repetition? End of verse 15 — '. . . that everyone who believes in him may have eternal life. End of verse 16 — 'that whoever believes in him shall not perish but have eternal life.' It would be strange if Jesus repeated himself like that. He does not usually do that sort of thing.

That is not the main reason. Secondly, the word *for* at the beginning of verse 16, as I have said already, usually means 'indeed' or it is a kind of expansion or explanation of what has just been said. Did Jesus expand or explain what he had just said? Unlikely.

Third, from verse 16 onwards, there are no more personal pronouns used. Up to verse 15, you have got Jesus saying 'you' and 'I', and it is personal pronouns; but from verse 16 onwards, it is all impersonal, third person: 'they', 'he'. It is no longer 'I' or 'you'. The personal side of the conversation has stopped. That still would not decide it for me. The next bit of evidence is this: Jesus always called himself 'Son of Man'. He never called himself 'only-begotten Son'. That is a title that John used for him, but Jesus never used it himself, yet in verse 15 he

says '. . . the Son of Man must be lifted up', and earlier,
'. . . the Son of Man came down from heaven'. If Jesus
is still talking, he would have said, '. . . for God so loved
the world that he gave the Son of Man . . . .' But he does
not say that. In verse 16, it changes to the only-begotten
Son, which is the title that John gave Jesus in chapter 1
and goes on using of Jesus. It is John's title, not Jesus'
title for himself. But what finally clinches it totally for
me is this: in verse 15, the cross has not happened yet, but
in verse 16, it has. Do you see what I mean? The death
of Jesus is still future in verse 15 when Jesus is talking
to Nicodemus, but in verse 16, it is all in the past. 'God
loved the world so that he gave' . . . . Over and done with.
So verse 15 was said before Jesus died, and verse 16 after
he died. Therefore, verse 16 onwards is John's comment
on what he has just reported.

5

THE MESSAGE FOR CHRISTIANS

So what we are dealing with in verse 16 is not Jesus' words. This is the important point for me. I have said that neither Jesus nor the apostles ever spoke to unbelievers about the love of God. This would have been the only exception. If verse 16 had been spoken by Jesus to Nicodemus, he would have been speaking about the love of God to an unbeliever –which would have been proof that I was wrong – but in fact it is not.

So does it really matter who said it, whether it was Jesus or John? Yes, it matters a great deal. Partly, as I have already pointed out, because it would make Jesus talk about the love of God to an unbeliever, which he never did, but primarily because we must therefore ask why did John say this, and to whom was he saying it? This means that verse 16 must be treated differently.

And we must ask why John added this comment to the conversation with Nicodemus. Not all of the four Gospels were written for unbelievers. (I have made this point very strongly and fully in my volume *Unlocking the Bible*, and I would suggest that you read the chapter in it on John entitled, 'Why was John Written?') It is assumed that if 3:16 comes in a 'Gospel' it is part of the gospel for unbelievers. It is part of the good news, and therefore John 3:16 can be used in evangelism, since the Gospels surely are evangelistic. But they are not. Two of the four 'Gospels' were written for believers, two were written for unbelievers. And it is very important that we use the four Gospels in the way they were intended to be used. In fact, only one of them is called a Gospel and that is Mark's. John did not call this the Gospel of John; we have called it that. And I believe that has given us this misleading idea that it is written for unbelievers. Moreover, John's Gospel has been freely distributed in evangelistic enterprises as being the best Gospel to give to people. It is the worst Gospel to give to unbelievers. It is not a Gospel for unbelievers! I think that some only use it hoping that people will read as far as John 3:16. But I have never heard an evangelist preach from John chapter 1. Have you ever heard an evangelistic sermon based on the text 'In the beginning was the Word and the Word was with God, and the Word was God'? You try and preach that to a non-believer. It is facing him with what will seem to him to be an impossible belief straight away —the eternal pre-existence of Christ. That is not the best place to begin with an unbeliever. John's Gospel was one of the two written for believers.

Now I think I must explain this a bit more fully, because the idea that a 'Gospel' was not written for evangelism or for unbelievers is a new idea to many people. Mark and Luke were both written for unbelievers, and they are very good to give to a person who knows nothing about Jesus and wants to read about him. Mark is full of action —what Jesus did. Luke is full of words, what Jesus said, teaching such matchless stories as the prodigal son and the good Samaritan — everybody understands those. But Matthew was not written for unbelievers, it was written for young believers, and particularly young Jewish believers, and in the early church there were many young Jewish believers. It is fatal to give Matthew to unbelievers. Why? Because they will misunderstand it. Matthew has taken Mark and then collected together everything Jesus said about the kingdom of heaven into five blocks. The first we call the 'sermon on the mount' (chapters five to seven) which is about the lifestyle of the kingdom. Then there is the mission of the kingdom (chapter ten). Then you get the growth of the kingdom (chapter 13). Then there is the community of the kingdom (chapter 18). Then, finally, comes the future of the kingdom (chapters 24 and 25). Every word of those blocks of kingdom teaching is written for believers and is totally inapplicable to unbelievers. For example, when Jesus said in the sermon on the mount 'You are the salt of the earth', did that apply to unbelievers? Of course it did not. In the same block of teaching Jesus said, 'Blessed are you, when you are persecuted for my sake and the gospel's . . . .' Is that for unbelievers? Of course it isn't.

In fact, what you have in Matthew is teaching for those who have come into the kingdom and need to learn how to live in the kingdom —what the lifestyle of the kingdom is. Regrettably, many have taken Matthew and turned it into a social and political programme. Gandhi did that; Dostoyevsky the Russian did that; Martin Luther King did it, and turned this sermon on the mount into a political manifesto of non violent revolution. It is an abuse of scripture. Matthew is written for believers to know about the kingdom of which they are now part. The ethics of the sermon on the mount are impossible for unbelievers and they are not too easy for believers either, but they are written for believers.

Similarly, John's Gospel is written for older believers. Everything in it is directed to the believer, and the overall purpose of the 'Gospel' is very clear. We need to know a little of the background. John was the oldest apostle. (All the others had been killed, he was the only one to die of old age.) He is writing sixty years after he first met Jesus, and he is the apostle whom Jesus loved. It says that Jesus loved John more than all the others. He was the beloved apostle. And he wrote this book for a specific purpose. You know that it is very different from the other three Gospels. There are things missed out of John that are in the others: his temptations, for example. And there are things in John that are not in the others. Why is it so different? Because it is about who Jesus was. It is not about *what he did*, like Mark. It is not about *what he said*, like Matthew and Luke; it is about *what he was*. It is the inside story of Jesus; it is the story of his person rather than his work. And it is written for people who have been Christians many years. Its purpose is stated in chapter 20. There it says that if everything Jesus said and did were to be written down, the world could not contain the books that would be written. 20:31 reads, 'But these things have been written down so that you may go on believing that Jesus is the Christ, the Son of God, and that going on believing you may go on having life in his name.' [Present continuous tenses] 'That you may go on believing and go on living.' We have come across this before, haven't we, in verse 16 of chapter three. 'Go on believing to go on having eternal life.' And John wrote the whole Gospel to encourage people to go on believing in the person Jesus —that they might go on having life in his name. Not that you may *start* believing, or that you may *come to believe*, but that you may *keep on believing* and therefore *keep on living*.

Now that is the overall purpose, and the reason for that purpose we know from other sources. I will explain it for you. Right there in Ephesus a man set himself up as a Christian teacher, who was not teaching the whole truth. His name was Cerinthus and he was teaching the same as I mentioned Jehovah's Witnesses teach today: that Jesus was not fully God; that he was nearer God than us but not fully divine. That is why the Jehovah's Witnesses' Bible changes John 1:1. Instead of saying 'In the beginning was the Word, and the Word was with God, and the Word was God,' they give you their Bible which says 'In the beginning was the word and the word was with God and the word was *a* God. By slipping in that little word 'a' they have changed the whole thing.

John was fighting this twisted view that Jesus was somewhere in between man and God; that he was not fully man on the one hand, and he was not fully God on the other. The error to stand against at that time was the belief that he was not fully God. John wrote this book deliberately and specifically to underline that Jesus was really God. Centuries later, the church had to put it in a creed. I wonder whether you have ever wondered what it meant when you said, 'very God of very God'? That is what it meant — that Jesus is absolutely all that God can be. He is God, fully divine.

They used to carry John to the swimming baths in Ephesus when he was an old man. They took him there for a bath and would lower him in the water. If he looked across and saw Cerinthus in the same water he would shout, 'Get me out, get me out, get me out.' Why? Cerinthus was in the pool! John saw that this man was destroying the Christian faith, so he was a deadly enemy of the truth. The 'apostle of love' loved truth as well.

So John wrote this Gospel to counteract that heresy, and we can see how he did this. First of all, there are seven people in John's Gospel who declare Jesus to be divine; *seven witnesses*, and that is the perfect number, ranging from John the Baptist right through to Thomas – seven witnesses that Jesus is God. Then he picked *seven miracles*. Six of them do not even appear in Matthew, Mark or Luke, but they are seven of the most spectacular miracles you can possibly imagine, all but one of them far more spectacular than those in the other Gospels. The only one in common was feeding the five thousand, and that is pretty spectacular. Healing people who had been blind for forty years! All seven miracles are signs to John that the one doing them was (unqualifiedly) divine. And there are *seven statements* beginning with the name of God, 'I am'. They are not in any of the other Gospels: 'I am the good shepherd', 'I am the way, the truth and the life', 'I am the resurrection and the life', 'I am the bread from heaven', 'I am the door of the sheep', and on one occasion, 'Before Abraham was, I am'.

So John is telling the reader of seven witnesses that

Jesus was God, seven miracles that no man has ever done, and seven statements from Jesus about himself which are matchless. (More on this will be found in my book *Unlocking the Bible*.) John wrote his Gospel to believers, in effect begging them: Do not listen to false teaching; go on believing that he is the Son of God, and go on having life in his name. That is why he wrote verse 3:16. That verse is addressed to believers, and if you go on to read the verses after 3:16, you find that he is discussing with believers the result of Christ coming and being 'given'. He says the result is that judgement is already happening, because people love darkness rather than light. The fact that Jesus came, that God gave him, and the world is not accepting him, is the beginning of judgement already. He is discussing with *Christian* readers the whole matter. In other words, verse 16, since it is written by John, and said to the readers, is not to be thought of as Jesus talking to a non-believer, Nicodemus. It is a message for Christians.

So let me take this a bit further. If we take verse 16 out of its context and use it as a tool in evangelism, we are abusing the verse. We will leave wrong impressions. As I have already pointed out, we give the impression that the gospel begins with the love of God, but it does not. The gospel begins with the **righteousness** of God and the **offer of his righteousness** (cf. Romans 1:16–17). So as a summary of the gospel, John 3:16 is lacking. And it is obvious now why neither Jesus nor the apostles ever preached John 3:16, or at least the content of it. It tends to focus on the dying rather than the living Saviour, the cross rather than the resurrection, never mind his ascension to and return from heaven. The main problem of using 3:16 in evangelism is that it does not adequately tell people how to respond to the gospel. There is not a word here about repenting —not one word. There is not a word about being baptised; there is not a word in John 3:16 about receiving the Spirit. The problem with using a verse in evangelism that does not tell people how to respond in proper detail is that you get a simple decision which is not enough for a real change in life. The classic example of such an abuse of a verse is Revelation 3:20, *'Behold, I stand at the door and knock. If anyone hears my voice and opens the door, I will come in and eat with him and he with me.'* People say that this is about conversion. Jesus is knocking at the door of your heart, please let him in. That verse has been used in every evangelistic tract I have ever picked up, I think. I have thirty-six booklets on my shelves on how to become a Christian, which I read carefully before writing *The Normal Christian Birth*. Every booklet quotes Revelation 3:20. But the 'door' there is a church door; the verse is spoken to Christians who have lost the presence of Christ from their church meetings, and the good news is that it takes just one church member to get Jesus back into a church. That is good news, isn't it? It has nothing to do with being converted, but if you use it for enquirers you will not mention repentance, you will not mention baptism, you will simply say, 'Open the door and let him in'. Or, 'Invite Christ into your life'. The apostles never talked like that at all, but we talk like that because we take a verse and we think it has got the gospel in it. The real response to the gospel is what Peter said in Acts 2, when they asked, 'What shall we do?', and he said, 'Repent and be baptised, every one of you, for the forgiveness of sins, and you will receive the gift of the Spirit.' That is the verse we should use when we are telling people how to become Christians, not 'Open the door and let him in', or, 'Invite him into your life'. Those are euphemisms which do not convey the reality.

I do emphasise that John 3:16 had no mention of repentance or baptism, both of which are essential to coming into the kingdom. Why didn't John 3:16 mention repentance or baptism? The answer is very simple. The people he is writing to have repented and been baptised. They no longer need that message. What they do need to hear is: *Go on believing, that you may go on having life*. It is in line with the whole tenor and purpose of the Gospel that John 3:16 does not deal with the basics of how to become a Christian. It is not dealing with a gospel situation, and outward evangelistic thrust. It is dealing with a very much more important message for Christians: Keep on believing.

As we look finally at the use and misuse of John 3:16, we have seen that when we make it an evangelistic message or a verse for unbelievers we tend to give them too simple a view —both of the gospel and of how to respond to it. We have noted that John does not mention repentance or baptism precisely because he is addressing those who have already repented, already been baptised, and need to be held to the faith they had at the beginning, and to go on believing and to go on having eternal life.

Now the biggest problem with making John 3:16 an evangelistic message for the unbeliever is that you lose sight of its important message to the believer, because that is why it was included in John's Gospel. The Gospel was written precisely to *keep people believing* so that they could *keep on having life*. Now perhaps one of the most common misconceptions is that eternal life is a package that has been transferred to us when we believed in Jesus so that *we now have this package*, we now have eternal life and we've got it for keeps, and we have got it for ever. The notion that you can *lose* eternal life is very new to many, many Christians, because the majority in this country have been told that you cannot, and that once you have got eternal life you have got it eternally, and that is settled for ever and ever. So often we are reading John 3:16 with a prejudiced mind, a mind that says 'once believe, always believe', or 'once saved, always saved'. So we read the tenses differently. Instead of realising it says 'God once loved . . .', and, 'If we go on believing, we go on having life', we switch the tenses back to front, and say, 'God goes on loving, and we only need to believe once.' So we have reversed the message because we have been reading it through certain spectacles. The message of John 3:16 (read as carefully as possible) is that eternal life can be lost, and you can cease to be having eternal life by ceasing to believe in him who died for us.

Now the reason for this is explained elsewhere in John's Gospel, and indeed in his first letter. There is just one verse in his first letter which gives a flood of light on this:

God has given us eternal life, and this life is in his Son. He who is having the Son is having life and he who is not having the Son is not having life (1 John 5:12).

'Having' is in the present continuous tense. The key there is that God has given us eternal life but this life is not in us. This life is in his Son; we are only given that life in his Son. We are not given it in ourselves. Therefore, as John goes on to say, *he who is having the Son*, or literally, *he who goes on having the Son*, goes on having life. But he who *does not go on having the Son* does not go on having life. Eternal life is not in the Christian, it is in Christ.

The passage in John's Gospel which makes that abundantly clear is John 15, where Jesus says 'I am the vine'; 'I am the true vine'. And he says, 'You are the branches', but the analogy breaks down, in that for Jesus the branches have a choice to stay in the vine or not. Normally in a vine the branches have no choice, they are in the vine and that is that. But in the living vine, the true vine, Jesus, the branches have a decision, a choice, to make. The choice is whether to stay in the vine or not. Therefore he exhorts the disciples: 'Abide in me' or, 'Reside in me', or, quite literally, 'Stay in me'. In other words, quite clearly we have a choice, even in Christ, either to stay in him or not to stay in him. Note the cost of not staying in him is this: that the branch has no life in itself. Its only life is in the vine. The branch does not have life, the vine has life, and the branch has life while it stays in the vine. But when it loses contact with the vine, what happens? Well, it withers. It becomes fruitless first, then it withers, and then it is cut off and burned. Strong language indeed, to Christian branches in the true vine. Yet Jesus is saying it as clearly as he possibly could: Stay in me, hang in there. And because the eternal life is in me and not in you, if you go on in me then you go on having life; if you don't stay in me you will lose life.

So eternal life is not a 'package' but a relationship, not a thing that God gave me when I believed; it is something I have when I am in Christ, and while I stay in Christ I go on having eternal life —and that is why John wrote this whole Gospel to Christians. Go on believing in him and you will go on having life. And that is the message of John 3:16 to believers. But as long as we are preaching it as a gospel for unbelievers we fail to warn believers of the possibility of losing eternal life by not staying in the true vine — by not abiding in Christ; by not going on trusting and obeying him; by not going on believing in him, and therefore not going on having life.

This life, John tells us, is not in us, this life is in Jesus. God has given us eternal life, but the package is wrapped up in him, not us; and it is in him that we receive the gift and outside of him we will lose it. So we have this urgent appeal. I am afraid it does mean that John 3:16 by itself challenges the cliché 'once saved, always saved', which is a cliché you have never found in your Bible. I am not even 'once saved' yet! I will be one day, when I am saved from all trace of sin whatever. On that day I will be in a position to shout, 'Once saved, always saved!' —because then it will be true. But I believe John had this deep burden in him: he could see Christians drifting away, led astray by false teaching about Jesus himself.

The verse 'How shall we escape if we neglect so great a salvation?' (Hebrews 2:3) is addressed to Christians, not unbelievers. It is not unbelievers neglecting the gospel there, it is believers neglecting their way of salvation. It is so easy to drift, to let faith just come down a peg or two, to fall into unbelief and to lose eternal life. The tragedy of using John 3:16 as a gospel message is that its true message is then lost. People take 3:16 and throw it at their unconverted neighbours, saying, 'That's for you.' It isn't. It is for all of us who are Christians.

6

APOSTLE OF WRATH

We have already noted that John has been termed 'the apostle of love'. Even John himself calls himself the 'beloved disciple', and he was. John was closest to the Lord at every meal. They did not sit on chairs, they reclined on a couch. You reclined on your left and you ate with your right hand, so of course your head was next to the feet of the next person. (Which is why they washed their feet before meals, which seems very sensible.) It meant that each person was leaning up against somebody else and John was always the one to lean up against Jesus. (Our expression 'bosom pal' goes back to the days when you literally leaned against somebody.) It was the chosen place, the right hand of the chief host, and John was always in that position. We have some idea as to what the other apostles felt about that. There was a bit of jealousy, which comes out at one point.

So John was the beloved apostle, and as he became older he became more and more emphatic about this word 'love'. In fact, as an old man, whenever he was asked to contribute in the Sunday worship he always would say, 'I have only one thing to say: my little children love one another.' It was said that he had many texts but one sermon for the last part of his life: love, love, love. He was the apostle of love, and there are many New Testament scholars who feel that the apostle John brings Christianity to its peak, that his writings are the pinnacle of New Testament Christianity, and that his emphasis on love was really the climax of all the New Testament teaching. Of course, he was the one apostle who said 'God is love' and from one point of view that is the most sublime and profound statement of divine nature that you could make. As a student in Cambridge I encountered that view, and you too may have come across preachers who hold strongly to this position.

Now I find it very interesting that John was not allowed to have the last word in the New Testament. If he really was the climax of it all, if he really was leading us to the heights in this strong emphasis on love, would it not be nice if the New Testament finished there, leaving us all with this picture of a God of love and our love for him and our love for each other? —in one sense, a very nice finish. But that is not how the New Testament finishes. Jesus has the last word in our New Testament, and his last word is a very strong word. From many points of view it seems like an unloving word. The Book of Revelation could hardly be described as a 'loving' book. The word 'love' only occurs once in the whole book where Jesus says to one of the seven churches, 'Those I love, I reprove and discipline.' Not a very 'nice', 'loving', 'comforting' thing to say. That is the only mention of the word 'love', and the rest of the book is about the wrath of God and the wrath of Jesus. Indeed, it reaches a climax in the middle, where people are praying for an earthquake to happen. Praying for earthquakes! Under what circumstances would people do that? You find that it is due to the fact that people realised they are looking at the angry faces of God the Father and God the Son. And rather than face their anger, they are crying: Mountains, fall on us, hide us from their anger. A 'loving' book? Yet it is the last word in the New Testament. It is the true climax to the story. Here is the irony of it— Jesus may have said to himself: Now who shall I dictate this book to? Who shall I give this terrible message to? I know, the apostle John; I'll give it to him. John was taken away, as an old man, to work in the quarries on an island called Patmos, and there the Lord Jesus gave him the revelation of what was to come and how it was all going to end —with a new universe wherein righteousness dwells.

Somehow this balances up the picture. The 'apostle of love' who so emphasised love in his Gospel and in his letters, was nevertheless chosen to give us the most dreadful news about God's future anger as he deals with the corrupt world. We need to be sure to get the whole truth across to people. The Lord Jesus chose the 'apostle of love' to write down this stark and stern warning, the Book of Revelation, to complete the story.

I have noticed that those who are today preaching a 'gospel of unconditional love' cannot handle the Book of Revelation, they shy away from it. They talk about the present rather than the future. Somehow the Book of Revelation does not fit in with their 'gospel'. But, to me, the whole thing fits together amazingly. The whole story began with God and it ends with God. All the way through it is an emphasis on the *God of righteousness* —he wanted a *righteous* world, and he intends to have it; and one day he will have a new heaven and a new earth wherein righteousness dwells. (2 Peter 3:13).

POSTSCRIPT AND PRAYER

In this study, we have looked very carefully at John 3:16. I now ask you to think about it for yourself. Do not 'play me off' against other teachers: 'Well, I agree with this teacher', or 'I disagree with . . . ', or, 'He doesn't agree with him'. That is a game we should not play. Search the scriptures for yourself. Look into them, be convinced by them, and speak the truth in love.

Let me make it quite clear that I believe we are to *show* people the love of God. We are to *show* people the *agape* of God, but we are not to preach it to them.

We are to bring them to the point where they realise that God is righteous, that everything he does is good and right, and that he will judge all of us without any favouritism or partiality — *and that we therefore need to go and look at the one hanging on the stake on the hill as God's loving action, to set us free from the certain death that will be ours otherwise.*

I suppose in the end it would be better for a person never to have been born than to miss the opportunity that God's loving gift of Jesus made possible.

God commends his love to all of us, in that while we were still sinners Christ died for us (Romans 5:8).

PRAYER

Lord, we have come to appreciate just a tiny bit of your love, that you should even pay attention to us in our need. What is man that you are mindful of him —that you should act on our behalf that one amazing time when you gave your Son for us? We are so grateful. Thank you that we have heard the good news, thank you for those who bothered to tell us. Thank you that your Holy Spirit gave us to understand. Thank you that you convinced us of sin and righteousness and judgement. Thank you that you made it possible.

I pray now that your Holy Spirit will teach us the truth we need to hear; if we are puzzled, may he make it plain. If we are confused, may he bring clarity out of confusion, order out of chaos, as he did at the beginning.

Lord, help me to think not about a particular author but about your word and your agape love.

Help us Lord, guide us, forgive us that we have been telling people that you love them unconditionally, without realising how they would understand that. But Lord, from now on, give us wisdom, courage and grace to tell them the truth, the truth that will set them free.

And to you we shall be careful to give all the glory and the praise and the honour that is due to your holy name, through Jesus Christ our Lord. *Amen.*